I am safe,
I am calm,
I am in control

With each
breath,
I release tension
and invite peace

I trust in my
ability to handle
whatever comes
my way

My mind is a place of tranquility & harmony

I let go of worry
and embrace the
present moment

I am capable,
strong, and
resilient

I choose peace over worry and courage over fear

I am surrounded
by love and
support

I am worthy of
inner peace and
happiness

I release the need
to control everything
& surrender to the
flow of life

I breathe in
calmness &
breathe out
tension

I trust that
everything is
unfolding for my
highest good

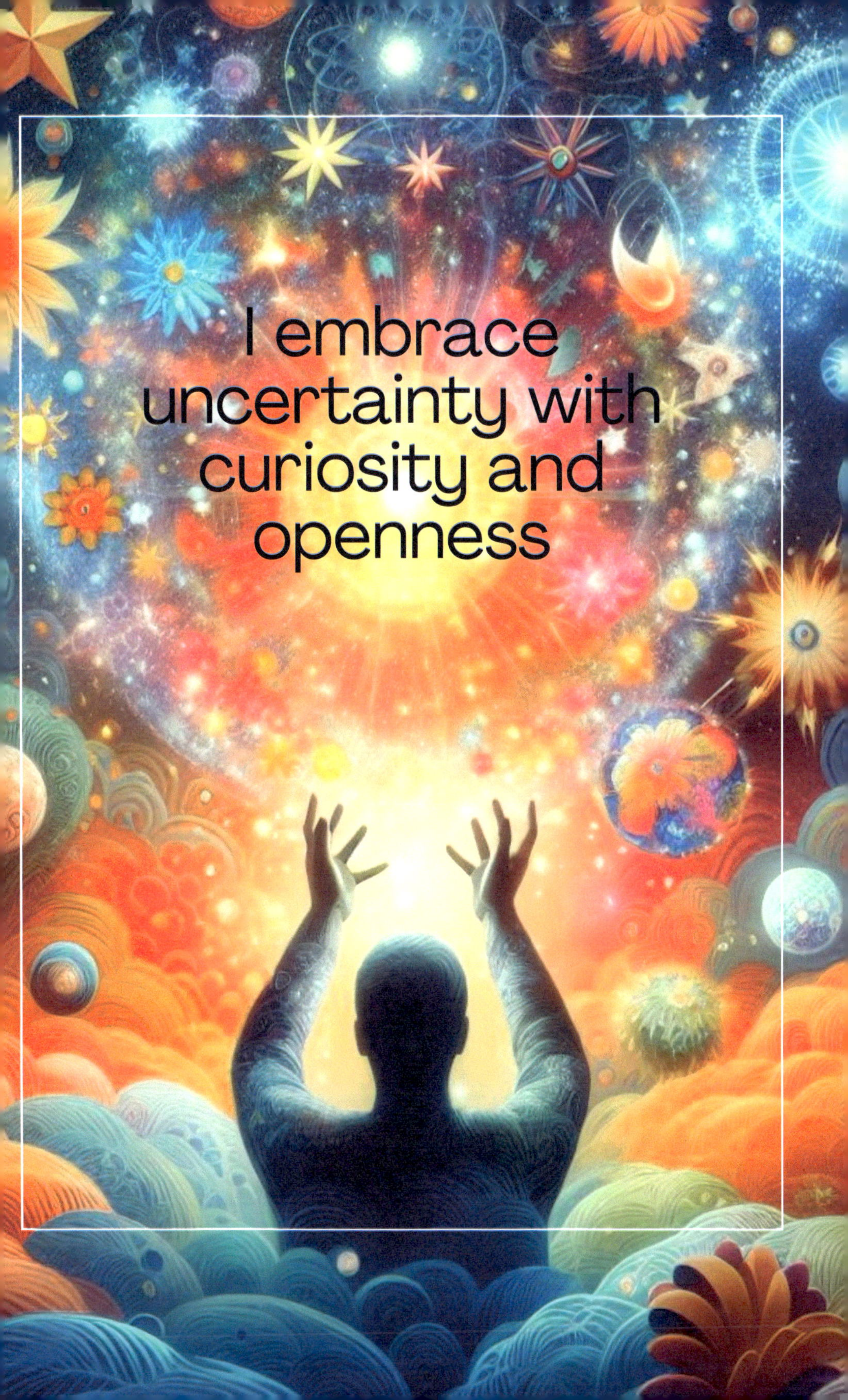
I embrace uncertainty with curiosity and openness

I am enough,
just as I am

I am the
architect
of my own
happiness

I release the past
and embrace
the beauty of
this moment

I choose thoughts that nourish and empower me

I am resilient,
resourceful;
capable of
overcoming
any challenge

I let go of perfectionism and embrace imperfections with love

I am surrounded
by positivity &
abundance

I am worthy
of love,
happiness, and
inner peace

I trust myself
to make the best
decisions for my
well-being

I release the need for approval and validation from others

I am a magnet
for miracles
and blessings

I choose to focus
on what I can control
and let go of
what I cannot

I am supported
by the universe
in every step
I take

I am resilient
in the face
of adversity

I am worthy
of all the good things
life has to offer

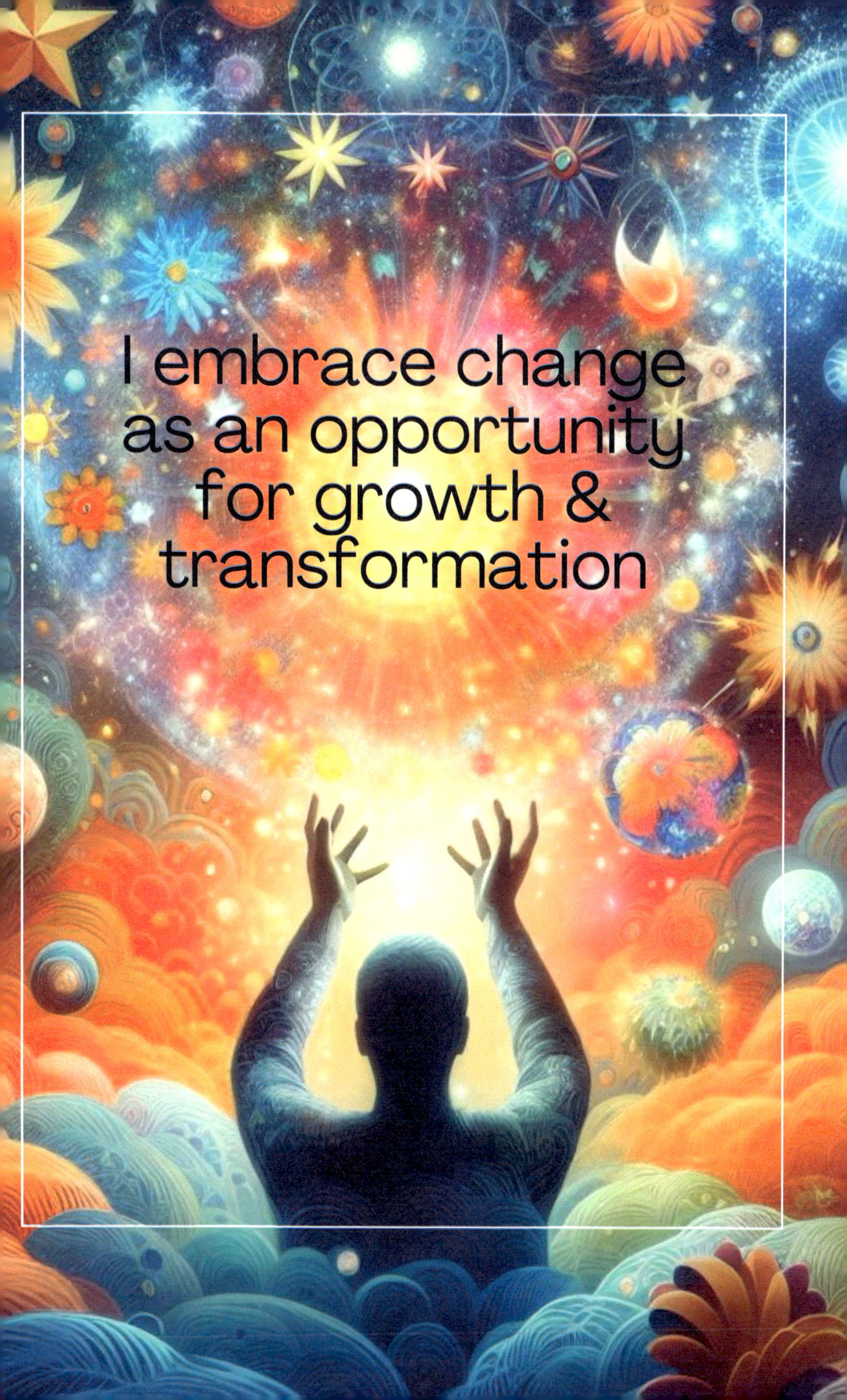
I embrace change as an opportunity for growth & transformation

I am at peace
with who I am,
where I am,
where I'm going

Made in the USA
Columbia, SC
21 May 2024

36028831R00035